THIS JOURNAL BELONGS TO

WELCOME TO THE LONELY WOODS

It is as sure as sunrise, as certain as sunset, that all who incarnated into this form will go through times when we feel very alone. We beings have evolved over thousands upon thousands of years within ancestral clans and tribes, defined by a river, a valley, the crops and the soil. We have connected through shared beliefs, values and customs, in cycles that circle around, over and again, until they are a part of our very being. We long for collaboration, shared experiences, understanding, and being a part of a family.

Even within those close-knit clans, we also yearned for time alone. In Nature. Deep in caves. To wander and walk. To be silent. In the heart of the forest. This aloneness was a journey of the soul, taken to come to self-knowledge and wisdom.

Then, aloneness could be a holy thing.

In today's world, for many of us, the sacred meaning of this choice to be in solitude for a time, has almost been lost. Yet, just as much as our souls crave belonging, our souls long for solitude.

Within these pages, you can begin to share the fruits of your purposeful aloneness with yourself. Let's transform our loneliness into sacred solitude, rich with connection and epiphanies of the spirit.

Within the space and peace of sacred solitude, we can deeply reflect, and renew our spirits. We can be offered wonder-filled discoveries – insights and inspired understanding of self. When we have the opportunity to reweave our energy with those of other beings like ourselves, we can do so without a need for being defined or approved of because we know who we are, and we trust in our selves. When we do this, we find a shining authenticity in partnerships that are human, inspired by Nature, and with those beyond the world of the seen.

Treasure your solitude. Become intimate with being in the presence of your own unique, shining essence. With being alone.

And if you find yourself feeling isolated or surrounded by many yet understood by few, this beautiful journal is your sanctuary in which to explore the deep mystery of existence. This journal will encourage you to enter into the deep communion of yourself with your soul, which in turn inspires an overflowing, ecstatic connection to spirit, and the freedom to explore the wonder of all-that-is.

Your life is precious, and rare, and wild. You are the very fabric of the universe, stitched of earth, air, fire and water into the form you are right now. Inside of you are constellations, fields of flowers, mountains of strengths, depths of ocean. You are never truly alone.

There are those who watch over you. Those who guide you. There are those who protect you. As you write, you will begin to feel their presence. You will unfurl and open and become ready to receive the gifts of solitude. Finally, you will hear the song of your soul.

Blessed be,

Blessed be, lonesome traveller. You are a wise one, setting out now on the pilgrimage of the soul, travelling alone into the Lonely Woods for a time...

Know now that seclusion can be an opportunity to recover your true heart's desire. There, in the stillness, your inner voice emerges.

In solitude, we become utterly ourselves again for a while, to meet no needs but our own – something so few of us can experience regularly.

Beneath the layers of conditioning,
our soul hungers for the solitary experience.

Wise ones know that time alone can be time very well spent.

Solitude may offer us solace, help us develop great resilience, and enable us to create a sense of connection that no longer relies upon being with others.

When we have a rich reservoir of time alone,
we come to learn that some of the troubles we carry are not ours.

Thanks to solitude, you may come to know which of your troubles to keep, which to learn from, and which you will always remember.

In solitude, we learn which burdens can be put aside, acknowledged as no longer ours to carry, and we can finally, truly, let them go.

In communion with yourself, your ability to change, adapt and recreate your life grows strong, and you can come to respect your resilience, your playful nature, your natural optimism.

Turn away from the voice of the world and listen instead to the wisdom of the growing world.

Once you hear the voice of Nature, even when you are seemingly alone, all will blossom, be enriched, become verdant once again.

You can make a wasteland a paradise.
Focus on sowing the seeds from which blessings can come forth.

When we are alone, we learn how to not take our inspiration or sustenance from others.

We do not drink from another soul's well.

We do not feed from another soul's cauldron.

We do not require anyone else's energy to generate our own.

All you have is within.

Within you is the spring — drink from it,
so the thirst of your spirit is quenched.

Within you is the air — open up to the north star that guides you from above.

Within you is the garden — water it so it grows.

Within you is the fire — stoke its passionate flame.

Within you is the earth – ground yourself within its support.

Find the source within you. Do not seek inspiration elsewhere — this is not the time for that connection. All you require lies within you.

Now is the time to follow your own path.
Do so until you discover the grail of the self and become your own light.

You are seen, beautiful soul.

Your isolation sometimes leads you to feel as though your existence will go unobserved. You are not invisible.

You are seen, and loved, even in moments of absolute aloneness.

The eyes of the spirit world watch over you
— more closely now than ever before.

The spirit beings, who dwell within all the elements, in every tree, in every breeze, within the deep and good earth, see you and wish to guide you.

Although you may feel loneliness, you have guardians helping you with what you need to know. Deepen your relationship with the true nature of this beautiful world.

We must step outside our relationships with others from time to time to nurture our relationship with ourselves.

What you are experiencing does not have to be loneliness.

Perhaps being alone is the true, deep, sacred work of becoming yourself.

Well spent solitude is filled with the beckoning yearning to know the world on your own terms.

Become an island. Offer the gift of solitude to your deepest self, and experience the world through the unfiltered truth of the self you are still becoming.

If we bend and twist the self to please others, we show only glimpses of who we are, hiding most of our selves, all for fear of rejection.

Step out into the light to see who is drawn to the truth of who we are.

Begin, in this moment, to deepen the love of your own ways.

Cease to speak words that appease others, yet offend your soul.

Offer a limitless level of care and love to your own self.

Who could you become if you already loved who you are?

*Some friendships withstand distance, time apart,
and even enforced separations. These are true friendships.*

We must set our course, even if it means our paths may divert from those we love for a while.

You must trust that, in time, paths that are destined to meet will merge as seamlessly as two rivers flowing into one, sometimes parting again, sometimes united until they empty into the great ocean of the life beyond this life.

Let the moments of genuine connection flow, and know those who truly love you will simply reach out a hand, open their arms, or even dance within the space only your two energies combined can create.

A time to be with others will come again. Know that, and know their souls are helping you to find them again, even amidst the darkness of the Lonely Woods.

*Foolish, they say, for you to choose to walk this strange path.
Isolation will become your only companion, they say, as you take
those first steps on the lonesome road that leads to your own true self.
These voices of doubt are illusions.*

This is no adventure, no indulgence, no needless seeking.
This is a pilgrimage of the soul.

There will be moments where your only companion is the voice inside your head. And that is the point. For when you hear that voice clearly for maybe the first time, listen.

*With every lonesome footstep, watch the path become smoother,
more encouraging, overflowing with love for all things,
filled with the peace of being in love with your life.*

Your inner light will illuminate the path, revealing to you the stony ground, the loose rocks, the thorns and ditches along the way.

You have access to the seat of creation, the spark of existence, and the codes that hold the blueprints of who and what we are.

No one else can light your way. It is the light in your heart that will give you the greatest guidance when all about you falls into darkness.

The torch that you bear in the Lonely Woods will, in time, become the light that inspires others to take up their torches and follow the radiance of their souls.

You are the light that leads.

We can be different at night. It is liberating when the peace and silence, the stillness and strangeness, give us a chance to become something other than our daylight selves.

Night feeds the souls who dare to dream with eyes wide open.

Your soul craves the song of the night, for your midnight self to arise, for the unshown self to be made visible, for the tattered wings you've tried too hard to hide to finally be seen by those with eyes of magick.

The night will never be lonely again, for within it, you find yourself.

Sometimes the gulf between the old world and the world yet to come feels like a chasm. It doesn't feel possible to bridge that gap, to somehow make it to the other side. Hold on...

Just at a point of resignation, a sign will appear... the scent of flowers, birdsong, the colours of dawn will give birth to hope in your heart.

When crossing a deep river, with all its undercurrents, trust and observe. The patterns and the safer spaces will become clear – if you watch closely. Suddenly the waters you must cross do not seem so deep, and within a shorter while than you think possible, the old and the new will be bridged, and you will flow into the next life within this lifetime.

Death walks amongst us.
Within every breath and every step dwells the mortality so many deny.

Do not fear endings.

Honour those who have left your life, or their own, with ceremony, ritual, and respect. Memory will make them immortal.

Learn to live with the truth — that death is not a fearful enemy but a gateway to another life.

The greatest death is a life unlived.

Your soul has lived through so many forms already.
But before you can transform again, we must pass through the
great gateway and allow our souls rest and freedom for a time.
Only then can we choose wisely the next journey on the path of the soul.

We sculpt our lives until their shapes are familiar, and we create patterns and stories and rituals around these shapes, all of which make up the beautiful moments of our days.

Our life is a whole world — and yet sometimes that world, through no decision we have made, comes to its ending, and all that once was will soon be the past.

Every living being is in flux and change.

Learn to let what is gone, go.

Take a moment to look upon what once was, to give it honour, to say goodbye. Then we stumble into the mysterious unknown, which holds what will become the beautiful future.

If you are deep in the Lonely Woods, know there will again come a time when you will share experiences, their pleasures amplified because they are mutual.

One of the true joys of companionship and friendship is the sense that the world is seen and experienced and even understood for a small moment by two or more people.

All is sweeter because the deep longing to share with another will be fulfilled, finally.

There will be times when the sensation of the air, the scent of the bud, the song of the bird, the wisdom of trees, the knowledge of the steady earth beneath your feet, and the solitude feels blissful.

The hermit is truly never alone,
for the Divine shall become their faithful companion.

There will be days when you are so overflowing with the song of the world that you will become one with the rhapsody of life.

What once was a void can become a world overflowing with delight and discovery.

There is an ecstatic communion that can never be experienced amidst the crowded life. But within your isolation, it opens to you.

There are gifts here on the lonely path. Receive them, and make them yours.

Sometimes it is when we are alone that we can be most true and real.
We live without artifice or the need to please or be pleased.
Finally free, we can simply be.

Do not make of your liberty a burden.

Call back to yourself the wandering parts of your mind and soul that departed when they knew others could not understand them.

Come together, be reunited within yourself, and feel the multitude of you.

You are a unique being, experiencing multiplicity through the oneness of your being.

Let being alone for a time heal and bring you back from the dark place that is loneliness.

The comforting, healing qualities of solitude are yours
— and these arrive spontaneously, unscheduled, without artifice.

You now truly love your own company.

The healer's touch may feel far from you, but if you allow the ancient ones to come to your aid, you will feel a tender hand upon your brow, offering you the energy of the Universe.

Allow yourself to be restored by the ancient and invisible forms of blessing and healing, even if human hands are far away right now.

Imagine... close those weary eyes... know the ancient ones are with you and let them reweave the fibres of light that make you into the being of radiance you so truly are.

Being alone for a time can mean we start to understand far more deeply what our stories have become – and we begin to know how our stories need to change.

The tale of your life now becomes more and more clear, written by your own hand, without all the suggestions and interruptions of others – even those that are well-meant.

Let the truth become clearer and clearer, until it is in front of you.
This truth is that your life is your story. And it is yours alone to write.

There will be times when being alone can make us feel so very small and full of doubt. Questions mutter into the ache of our being: Do I matter? Do others care? Why do I feel so lost? Do not still these voices. Instead, comfort them.

At first, the vastness of the silence that can greet our existential questions may seem to confirm our insignificance. This is an illusion.

As you walk the Lonely Woods, you will begin to feel a belonging, as if you fit within a greater design. A divine plan.

You are significant, for you are a child of this planet, and you belong here.

It seems lonelier at night, somehow. Make friends with the darkness.

In darkness, we become strange as moonlight.

By entering the void of night, you bring your magickal self to life.
The dawn will come.

Let the night's peculiar light illuminate the wild world that resides within you.

What was once unseen will reveal itself and share the road with you, enriching every day with its divinity.

So often, we are distracted. We plough through the day, too busy to see or hear, to feel and to think. And the deep soul starves within us.

The key to moving into a more soulful and rich connection with yourself and the world lies within how you use the gift of these more lonesome times.

Within the cocoon of your own company, you will have moments of realisation that are the key to your entire life taking a different shape in the days to come.

Soul memory is a kind of well, the deep reservoir of the ancestors,
which is where longed-for parts of your self and soul live,
patiently awaiting you to find them.

Gaze into your well of memory. Conjure up the lost selves.
Up they rise, to rejoin you again.

Give the unknown within you the space to share its wise stories with you. Nothing that belongs to you can ever be lost.

It is only for a time that you forgot the blessings of all that you are.
With remembrance comes rebirth.

Even though the time has passed for your tales to intertwine,
the loosening of the bonds of love need not be bitter.

You will not be lost when you follow the darkening path into the unknown.

Trust that the light you carry within is the light you have ignited for others.
These lights will be the guides on the mysterious path before you.

Endings open the space for beginnings. Because you let go, a beginning is on its way, made more magickal and beautiful because you made space for it.

The self that held on so tight had no space to receive.

You now know that when you let go, a sacred space is made,
and into that space will walk the wonder.

There is one who has always watched over you, compassionate and sage,
but never interfering with your free will.

To know you have this guardian is to understand that, while although there is loneliness, you are never alone.

You have one who watches over you, one who is linked to the path of your soul, from your first breath to your last, and they will be with you in the great in-between of your lifetimes.

The one who watches over you knows the sacred quest of your soul, and when it sees that you have lost your way, they will come to you in blessed ways to remind you to go on.

Your soul knows the way.

Soon will come a reunion, a beautiful homecoming — a time of enrichment and contentment. The solitude you have experienced means you have more to share, more than ever before.

Because of your transformation, a gift of solitude, your true soul companions shall see you, understand you, accept you, love you, reach for you in the morning, and kiss you as you fall asleep.

These times of solitude shape your soul.
And the shape it has taken is beautiful indeed.

Your unfelt emotions, the mysteries of the psyche, the flowing nature of who you are fearful to be — all these mysteries can now be explored.

Sink into the unknown, and know it is safe for you to be within this watery place of emotional mystery.

Feel the gift of the silence, the calm, the weightlessness, and the depth of this subterranean world, the mystery of the Lonely Woods.

You are a part of the Lonely Woods, just as you are a part of the human world. It can become your sanctuary and a healing grove.

The beauty of the lonesome path will open your eyes
to the beauty of the yearnings within you.

Take comfort in knowing there are others like you,
and in time, your paths may meet.

Others like you are experiencing an awakening.

The truth you are awakening to is that even at the centre of your being, there is change. You endlessly give birth to yourself, living life within life, within life.

It seems as if you are the only one experiencing such a profound rebirth, and this can lead you to feel bleak, believing that there is no one else who has experienced quite what you have. This is not true.

You are undergoing an initiation,
one your soul has requested and agreed to undertake.

Your soul knows that hard as this great initiation can seem, the rewards will come, lifetime after lifetime. This is worth it. In this way, your soul has fulfilled its quest.

It is true that your experience is unique and profound. But it is also true that there are other souls gently seeking the possibilities of their own freedom.

Many brave souls are walking their own paths, shunning the loud voices of the human world that shout their empty words into numb ears and blank minds.

There are others like you.
You are not alone in this rebirthing of the inner and outer worlds.

Even in the Lonely Woods, true communion comes in the moments where two, who once felt like strangers, connect over the simple delight of the warmth that springs up between them.

Our souls, for all that they grow in solitude, crave those moments of connection. And here you have this moment.

If you find yourself entwined with another blessed soul, let all unfold in time. For now, rest a while in the bliss of this communion.

The tender part of you and a dear soul-friend have found a safe place, each within the other.

Nurture friendships, gently and with respect.

Have patience when you meet a kindred spirit. Destiny is an unfolding. It cannot be hurried. In time, you will learn what you are meant to be to each other. For now, rest a while in the bliss of this communion.

When you find others who have found kinship and contentment,
learn of their rites.

Which gifts could you share with others?

From this lonely time, even amidst it, will you make time for play, delight, and celebration in your life?

This is a time for the new, for the unlearned,
for the joyous discovery of what could be, and what will come.

Anticipate your rebirth with all the sweetness and calm trust you can muster, and learn from those who have found a way to live together, well.

A sweet, small blessing will open your energy to receive even more joy when in retreat from the world.

Destiny wishes you to be content, to feel loved,
and to see the wonder in every small thing this day.

Look about you — for right there, in the smallest of places, are the blessings you have been yearning for, yet missing.

Open your new eyes to the world — and what once went unseen and unappreciated can be truly known for the very first time.

It is time to rest alone awhile, beautiful soul.

Rest within a sanctuary.
This rest is when some of your most sacred work is done.

Linger in your dreams, in the cocoon you create as you separate from the exterior and enter deeply into the divine universe that dwells within you.

It is time to restore and regenerate, to recreate and reweave the inner world that sanctuary, the memory palace and beautiful grove where all true healing takes place.

While the world of Nature is a-resting, you too must return to the deep for this phase of the cycle of life. Slumber and dream, so you can emerge renewed.

When the reunion comes, it will be blessed, pure, and so full of joy that you will not regret the time that took you from the world.

The time to come will be so full of love and kindness, of recognition and support, it will transform all the days of your life.

Your life is becoming a tapestry woven of love. You are held, supported, seen, and heard. A reunion, this union of two renewed souls, is blessed.

Into the great, wide unknown you walked, and the Lonely Woods welcomed your broken soul, mending it with every unsteady step.

You have found a home even within the Lonely Woods,
and the path you are walking through this place is clear, brighter, higher.
Breathe in the air of freedom.

You, walker of the Lonely Woods, are more filled with joy and blessings than you could ever have imagined.

Walk on, bright soul, even deeper into the Lonely Woods,
and ready your heart for soaring joy.

Solitude can be a great blessing — born from the quiet, the stillness, the space around and within us.

And when you emerge and come back to yourself,
to those you love and to those who love you, you will be transformed.

The light within you is longing to be freed. It will not vanish, be stolen, or shrivel if you take it from its hidden place. Bring your light forth and let it lead.

You have been changed by your journey through the Lonely Woods.
You are the pure essence of your divine being. You are whole.
You are complete. You are radiant.

You have completed your quest
into the Lonely Woods.

YOU ARE REBORN.
AND YOU ARE FREE.